AMAZING ANIMAL SELF-DEFENSE

Gooey Slime
Gross Hagfish

by Rex Ruby

Bearport
PUBLISHING

Minneapolis, Minnesota

Credits: Cover and title page, © Brandon Cole Marine Photography/Alamy; Design elements throughout, © Veronika Oliinyk/iStock; 4, © Kevin Thirion/iStock; 5, © blickwinkel/Alamy; 6, © MediaNews Group/Orange County Register/Getty Images; 6–7, © ffennema/iStock; 9, © Doug Per-rine/Minden Pictures; 10–11, © Tom McHugh/Science Source; 13, © Wu, Norbert/Superstock; 15, © Ryan Somma/Flickr; 16–17, © Gina Kelly/Alamy; 18–19, © wildbillxlh56/Flickr; 21, © Wu, Norbert/Superstock; and 23, © Josephine Jullian/iStock.

Bearport Publishing Company Product Development Team
President: Jen Jenson; Director of Product Development: Spencer Brinker; Senior Editor: Allison Juda; Editor: Charly Haley; Associate Editor: Naomi Reich; Senior Designer: Colin O'Dea; Associate Designer: Elena Klinkner; Associate Designer: Kayla Eggert; Product Development Assistant: Anita Stasson

Library of Congress Cataloging-in-Publication Data

Names: Ruby, Rex, author.
Title: Gooey slime : gross hagfish / by Rex Ruby.
Description: Minneapolis, Minnesota : Bearport Publishing Company, [2023] | Series: Amazing animal self-defense | Includes bibliographical references and index.
Identifiers: LCCN 2022033638 (print) | LCCN 2022033639 (ebook) | ISBN 9798885093903 (library binding) | ISBN 9798885095129 (paperback) | ISBN 9798885096270 (ebook)
Subjects: LCSH: Hagfishes--Juvenile literature. | Animal defenses--Juvenile literature.
Classification: LCC QL638.14 .R83 2023 (print) | LCC QL638.14 (ebook) | DDC 597/.2--dc23/eng/20220715
LC record available at https://lccn.loc.gov/2022033638
LC ebook record available at https://lccn.loc.gov/2022033639

Copyright © 2023 Bearport Publishing Company. All rights reserved. No part of this publication may be reproduced in whole or in part, stored in any retrieval system, or transmitted in any form or by any means, electronic, mechanical, photocopying, recording, or otherwise, without written permission from the publisher.

For more information, write to Bearport Publishing, 5357 Penn Avenue South, Minneapolis, MN 55419.

CONTENTS

Goo, *Ew!* 4
Slime Time 6
Deadly Defense 8
Knot Now 10
Slip and Slide 12
On the Inside 14
An Ocean Home 16
Dig In 18
Baby Hagfish 20

Another Slimy Defense 22
Glossary 23
Index 24
Read More 24
Learn More Online 24
About the Author 24

GOO, EW!

While hunting for food, a shark spots a long, skinny animal moving back and forth. But it's not a slithering snake—it's a swimming hagfish! As the shark closes in to grab a meal, the hagfish does something surprising. It shoots out **slime**! The gooey stuff distracts the shark, and the hagfish escapes.

Hagfish are also known as slime eels.

SLIME TIME

A hagfish's body is always making slime. When the animal is in danger, white goo shoots out of tiny holes in the fish's skin. This goo mixes with ocean water and **expands**, turning into a big mess of thick slime.

Minutes after a hagfish shoots its goo, the fish has already made enough new slime to fill a five-gallon (19 L) bucket.

Deadly Defense

Slime from a hagfish can kill an enemy fish. How? The goo **clogs** the other fish's **gills**. This makes it hard for the animal to breathe. If the slimed enemy can't get the goo out of its gills fast enough, it will choke and die. That's why many ocean animals won't even try to eat a hagfish!

Seabirds, sharks, wreckfish, and seals are among the animals that do attack hagfish.

KNOT NOW

When a hagfish slimes an enemy, it also gets slime on itself. But the hagfish has a trick to get the goo that sticks to others off its own body. The long, thin fish ties itself into a knot! Then, it moves the knot from its head to its tail. This movement wipes off the slime.

> A hagfish also sneezes to get rid of any slime in its nose.

Nose

Slip and Slide

A hagfish's slime also helps it get food. The fish hunts for sick or dead animals on the ocean floor. When a hagfish locates its **prey**, it slimes itself. Then, its slippery body easily slides into the prey through any opening it can find—even the other animal's mouth.

A hagfish doesn't have eyes. It uses smell and its **feelers** to find a meal.

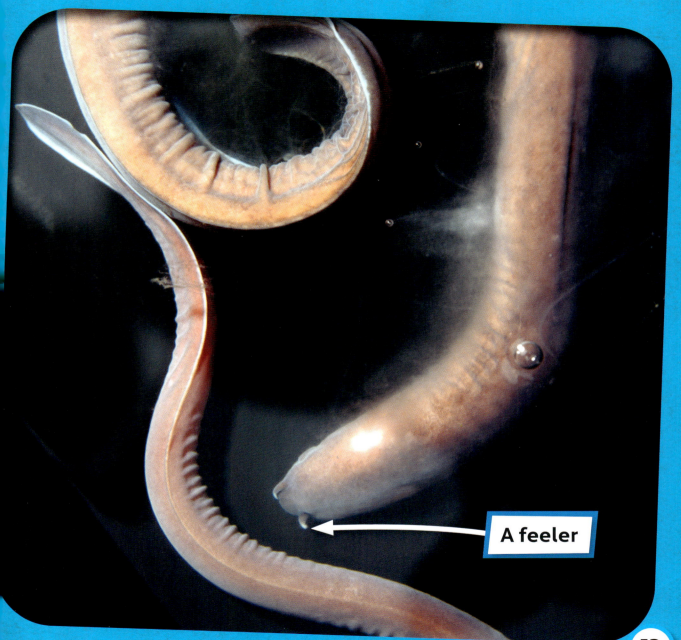

A feeler

On the Inside

Once the hagfish is in the prey's body, it starts to eat. This creature eats from the inside out! Since the hagfish doesn't have jaws for chewing, it sucks up its food. *Slurp!* When the hagfish is done, all that's left of the meal is skin and bones.

Hagfish don't always need to suck their food. They can also take in **nutrients** through their skin.

AN OCEAN HOME

There are about 70 different kinds of hagfish that live in oceans all around the world. Some kinds live in large groups, while others live alone. Most of them stay in cold waters near the ocean floor, where they can find food. They've been found nearly 9,000 feet (2,700 m) deep in the ocean.

Up to 15,000 hagfish may live together in one small part of the ocean.

DIG IN

Eating isn't the only thing these creatures do at the bottom of the ocean. Hagfish also make their underground **burrows** there. The animals push their bodies into the soft mud. The burrows don't last long, though. They cave in as soon as the hagfish leave.

Hagfish may find other safe spots by squeezing into small holes in rocks.

BABY HAGFISH

The mud on the ocean floor also gives hagfish a safe place to lay their eggs. When the eggs **hatch**, the baby hagfish look like their parents, only smaller. Soon, the babies will be ready to ooze their own gooey slime!

A mother hagfish can lay up to 30 eggs at a time.

ANOTHER SLIMY DEFENSE

CLOWN FISH

A clown fish is another sea creature that uses slime for safety. This fish is covered in slime. The slippery stuff protects it from getting stung by the sea anemone (uh-NEM-uh-nee) where the fish makes its home. The anemone can't tell the difference between its own slime and the clown fish's. So, it doesn't sting the little fish!

A clown fish in an anemone

GLOSSARY

burrows holes or tunnels animals make to live in

clogs fills up or blocks with something

expands gets bigger

feelers the body parts that stick out from a hagfish's mouth and help it find food

gills body parts that help fish breathe underwater

hatch to come out of an egg

nutrients substances such as vitamins or proteins that plants and animals need to stay alive

prey an animal that is hunted by another animal for food

slime a soft, slippery goo

Index

babies 20
burrows 18
clown fish 22
eating 8, 14
eggs 20
enemies 8, 10
feelers 12–13
knots 10
oceans 6, 8, 12, 16–18, 20
prey 12, 14
skin 6, 14
sneezes 10

Read More

Berne, Emma Carlson and Susan K. Mitchell. *Chemical Cover: Smells and Poisons (Animal Defense!)*. New York: Enslow Publishing, 2020.

Lawrence, Ellen. *Slime Crimes: Hagfish (Slime-inators & Other Slippery Tricksters)*. New York: Bearport Publishing Company, 2019.

Lundgren, Julie K. *Gross and Disgusting Animals (Gross and Disgusting Things)*. New York: Crabtree Publishing, 2022.

Learn More Online

1. Go to **www.factsurfer.com** or scan the QR code below.
2. Enter "**Gooey Slime**" into the search box.
3. Click on the cover of this book to see a list of websites.

About the Author

Rex Ruby lives with his family in Minnesota, far away from the ocean. He's happy that hagfish don't live in lakes!